Transition Into Organic Foods

by Rachel Valentin

This book is not a diet book. My sole purpose is to introduce people to organic foods and to share my experiences of the organic food market. Any definitions, similarity of words to articles, flyers or magazines are purely coincidental and should be regarded as such.

Printed and bound in the United Stated of America. All rights reserved. No part of this book may be reproduced or transmitted in any form or by any means, electronic or mechanical, including photocopying, recording, or by an information storage and retrieval system-except by a reviewer who may quote brief passages in a review to be printed in a magazine, newspaper, or on the Web-without permission in writing from the author.

For information please contact me at
TransitionIntoOrganicFoods@verizon.net

Transition Into Organic Foods
by Rachel Valentin

Copyright ©2004 Rachel Valentin

First printing 2004

ISBN 0-9753061-0-3
LCCN 2004-092007

Although the author and publisher have made every effort to ensure the accuracy and completeness of information contained in this book, I assume no responsibility for errors, inaccuracies, omissions, or any inconsistency herein. Any slights of people, places, or organizations are unintentional.

ATTENTION CORPORATIONS, UNIVERSITIES, COLLEGES, AND PROFESSIONAL ORGANIZATIONS:
Quantity discounts are available on bulk purchases of this book for educational and gift purposes. Please contact me at TransitionIntoOrganicFoods@verizon.net

Transition Into Organic Foods

CONTENTS

CHAPTER ONE: UNDERSTANDING ORGANIC 1
Organic Foods
Conventional Foods
Chemicals
Pesticides
Natural
Why Buy Organic

CHAPTER TWO: GETTING INTO ORGANIC FOODS . . . 13
Where to Start
Organic Oatmeal Raisin Cookies (Recipe)
Reading Organic Labels

CHAPTER THREE: NUTRITION AND HEALTH 25
Organic Foods and Ingredients

CHAPTER FOUR: BASICS 38

CHAPTER FIVE: EXERCISES FOR YOU 46

INTRODUCTION

This book came into existence because of my life's transformation and experiences. It all started with my saying "yes" to life, which later led to one of the best decisions I have ever made. I feel better eating foods with no chemicals; I enjoy sharing my experiences with others and helping people learn about organic foods. I want to share what I know about organic foods: how they are different from conventional foods; where to shop for organic products; what products are available; the cost; and so much more.

Not having the choice is the equivalent of not being able to know what is on the market, and this is what led me to write this book. I hope it will help you in your organic transition. And remember, you can do it!

Chapter 1: Understanding Organics

Organic Foods

Organic is the term used to describe food produce that is grown without the use of harmful chemicals, pesticides, synthetic preservatives, genetically engineered crops, and irradiation.

Conventional Foods

Conventional foods are grown with harmful chemicals, pesticides, synthetic preservatives, genetically engineered crops, and irradiation and are destructive to the earth.

Pesticides

Pesticides are chemical substances used to destroy insects and rodents; herbicides are chemicals used to kill weeds.

What are Antibiotics?

According to the Webster's New World dictionary, antibiotics are certain chemical substances produced by various microorganisms, specifically bacteria, fungi, and actinomycetes, (actinomycetes is a member of the bacteria family) having the capacity to dilute solution to inhibit the growth of or to destroy bacteria and other microorganisms.

Antibiotics, including penicillin streptomycin, and tetracycline, are used in the treatment of various infectious diseases. (Please refer to dictionary).

TRANSITION INTO ORGANIC FOODS

How are Conventional Foods Grown?

Conventional foods are grown differently from organic foods. The soils are filled with long-lasting chemicals and pesticides. The seeds or crops that are used to grow plants are genetically altered. Sewage and sludge are used as fertilizers. Herbicides or fungicides are used to destroy plant weeds. The reason some companies use chemicals and pesticides is because it is less expensive to use them (and yield fewer loss of crops) than not. This, in turn, gives them higher profits-but at the expense of our health. What is important to these companies is production, the fastest and cheapest means with less regard to safety and careful preparation.

How are Organic Foods Grown?

Organic foods are grown quite differently from conventional foods. Agricultural management is employed to enhance the earth's natural system. Seeds and crops are not genetically altered; harmful and long-lasting chemicals and pesticides are not used. Livestock management practices are implemented to promote healthy, humanely treated animals, providing the animals with clean air and allowing them outdoors. Chemicals are not used on animals, so we do not have to be worried about ingesting disease-causing chemicals ourselves. Chemicals are used only if an animal has an infection, and then if it is treated with antibiotics, the meat cannot be sold as organic.

Conventional and Non-organic – Are They the Same?

Yes. Conventional is the term used to describe foods treated with harmful chemicals. Non-organic is the term used to describe foods that are made with chemicals. So whenever you see these terms at organic and health food stores, you will know they mean the same thing.

Is Biogenetically Altered Food the Same as Organic?

Biogenetically altered food is not the same as organic. Organic foods are foods that are grown without the use of harmful chemicals and pesticides, whereas, biogenetically altered foods are foods in which the cells are split to produce more. So in actuality, we are interfering with the natural science of the foods, altering the growth structure so we can get more nutrients from the same plants or increase resistance to herbicides. This is not organic.

Is Organic the Same as Natural?

No, organic is not the same as natural. Organic, as described above, can either be made 100% without chemicals, or with at least 95% organic ingredients, or with at least 75% organic ingredients. The term natural is used when a product is made from natural plant products without the use of chemicals or a preservative synthetic. It does not have a label validating its accuracy.

Environmentally Sound Practices

Environmentally sound practices refer to practices that are in harmony with keeping the earth's natural balance. This includes not using harmful chemicals, pesticides, or growth hormones on plants and animals and allowing the animals to roam freely outdoors.

Why Buy Organic?

Chemicals and pesticides are harmful to us. They destroy and weaken the immune system. By being conscious of how our foods are being handled can add years to our lives.

How Does Organic Food Taste?

Organic foods taste better than conventional foods. When I was enrolled in a Certified Dietary Manager Program (CDM), as part of a taste test, my instructor had each class member bake a dessert to bring into class. I baked my favorite dessert: organic oatmeal raisin cookies. All my classmates loved them. My cookies got such great reviews, my fellow students just had to know what the recipe was. To their surprise, the cookies were made completely with 100% organic ingredients.

Recipe:

My Favorite Organic Oatmeal Cookies

1 1/2 cups	sifted all-purpose organic flour
1/2 teaspoon	baking powder
1/2 teaspoon	salt
1 cup	organic vegetable shortening
1 3/4 cups	firmly packed organic brown sugar
1	egg
3/4 cup	rice vanilla beverage or milk
1 3/4 cups	organic quick-cooking rolled oats
1 cup	organic raisins

Method:

1. Sift flour, baking soda, salt onto waxed paper
2. Cream shortening with brown sugar until brown sugar becomes fluffy in a large bowl; beating egg and milk.
3. Add dry ingredients, blending well to make a thick batter. Fold in rolled oats and raisins.

4. Drop by teaspoonsful, 3 inches apart, on greased cookie sheets.

5. Bake in moderate oven (375° F.) 12 minutes or until lightly golden. Remove from cookie sheets; Cool completely on wire racks. Makes about 3.5 dozen.

Please Note:

According to the USDA, salt and water are not labeled organic, so you can use what you've normally used.

You can substitute the rice vanilla beverage for organic milk.

Where Can I Buy Organic Foods?

Organic foods are becoming more and more available to customers; they can be purchased at farmers' markets and health food stores, and increasingly in conventional supermarkets too. If you would like to know more, you can visit: www.wholefoods.com, 1-888-746-7936 or www.wildoats.com, 1-800-494-9453 to find out where there is a store near you. Also, be aware that as the organic market grows, there will be more and more organic foods available at conventional supermarkets.

TRANSITION INTO ORGANIC FOODS

Why Does Organic Food Cost More?

Right now, organic food costs more because the process by which organic land is prepared requires the soil to be toxic-free for many years.

1. Preparing the land for planting organic foods take longer than planting conventional crops, because the land is prepared without the use of chemicals. Also, the soil preparation and other work are done by hand, with limited use of machinery.

2. Farmers use crop rotation to nourish the soil instead of using chemicals that quickly prepare the land for replanting crops as soon as they're reaped. In crop rotation, plants are moved around to another plot every year, rather than replanting the same crop in the same spot. For example, lettuce would be planted where the tomatoes were last year, and vice versa.

3. Acquiring land that has been chemical-free for at least three years is not very easy, because for many years land has been filled with harmful chemicals and pesticides.

4. Season change may play a part in the fruits being more expensive, just as occurs with conventional fruits.

Livestock Management

This refers to the handling of animals. Right now, it is not common practice to promote a healthy environment and humane conditions for livestock such as cows and chickens. For example, not enough fresh air and outside access. Mad Cow Disease was a result of such unhealthy livestock management. It becomes clear that after all the concerns with Mad Cow Disease, eating organically raised meat is safer.

Growth hormones are used to hasten the growth in beef cattle, which means the hormones used in the animals would end up in us. This is where we get all the negative effects of chemicals. Animals raised with chemicals have been known to cause all different types of diseases in humans, such as high blood pressure, liver and kidney damage, and certain types of cancer. There are several hormones used in animals which causes these diseases, estradils-17B, testosterone, progesterone and their synthetic analog

TRANSITION INTO ORGANIC FOODS

zerono, trenbolone acetate (TBA) and melengestrol acetate (MGA).

Chapter 2:
Getting Into Organic Foods

Where Do I Start?

If you have made a conscious decision to change your life-because this is your life we are talking about here!- then here are a few small steps you can take to switch from chemically filled foods to organics. Try first by changing your milk. There are so many chemicals in conventional milk.

Look at the selection of milk in your health food store. Browse the aisle and get familiar with what is on the shelves. There is a wide range to choose from, for example, there is organic whole milk, low-fat (1% and 2%), and lactose free; there's goat's milk, soy milk, pasteurized, and ultra-pasteurized. Do not be afraid to try something new, unless you have a health issue. Then you have to pay special attention to the items you buy, as you would have in the past with conventional foods. Please consult your physician.

Organic foods are available in all categories and cultures. I have listed some of the foods from different cultures that are available. You do not have to stop eating the foods you enjoy, because there is quite a selection. Gradually introduce yourself to your new way of eating, and over time you will see the changes and feel the difference in your body. Be adventurous.

One time when I was at an organic foods market picking up some items to make cookies, a woman on line behind me kept bending her head over, trying to see what I had in my hands. I looked back at her with a smile, and she asked me, "Going to make something good?" "Yes," I said, "organic cookies." She asked me how it tastes, so we began talking. I explained to her all the ingredients, and she said that must taste great, but she paused and a look of frustration came over her face. "I'm feeling very overwhelmed," she said. "All these organic products- I don't know where to start!" I told her keep it simple. Just substitute one product at a time. Don't do it all overnight. Try changing one ingredient or item a week. Start with milk!

When you prepare meals at home, keep in mind to have a variety of tastes, textures, and colors. It will be much more interesting and appetizing. When you set the table for yourself or your family or friends, make a nice presentation. You do not have to go overboard. Just nice and simple, so as to encourage them to try something new and to eat healthy.

As you work toward having a healthy lifestyle, aim for a healthy weight. By doing this, we can become more active every day. You may want to consult your doctor as to how much activity you should be doing. Let the food pyramid guide you in your quest toward organics unless you have health issues, please consult your physician.

Extra Firm: Great for stir-frying, grilling, and sautéing.

Meat analog

Meat analog is another soy protein product made to taste like meat. Several different flavors can be simulated, such as beef, pork, and chicken. It is sold as dried food or canned. It is made into "hamburger," "hot dog," and even in sliced "deli food" style. It is used the same as you would for picnics and barbecues.

Smart Dogs™

Smart Dogs are like hot dogs, except they are made from soy. One day my husband and I were out picking up a couple of items at the health food store, and we decided to try Smart Dogs. I was not sure if we were going to like it because one time, before I started eating organic foods, we tried a soy dog that was a different brand and did not like it. It had no taste and was not appetizing. Now, just a few years later, we have more choices and great-tasting ones like Smart Dogs.

What the Labels Mean

USDA: Stands for United States Department of Agriculture. They are in charge of the safety of meat, poultry and egg products.

FDA: Food and Drug Administration. They are responsible for ensuring that foods are safe, wholesome and sanitary. Several years ago the Nutrition Labeling and Education Act made changes to the food labels.

They allowed labels to carry the effects of health condition in relation to food and specific diseases. For example a diet rich in fiber containing grain products, fruits and vegetables can reduce the risk of some cancers. In 1994 food manufacturers were required to make labels easier for consumers to read.

TRANSITION INTO ORGANIC FOODS

Reading Organic Labels

Under the organic labeling, all products labeled as "organic" must be certified by a USDA-accredited certifying agency.

100% Organic

Excluding water and salt, products must contains only organically produced raw and processed materials.

Its certifying agent must appear on the label. Certifying seal may be used.

Organic

At least 95% of the ingredients are organically produced ingredients.

The percentage of ingredients may also appear on the label.

Its certifying agent must appear on the package. Certifying seal may be used.

Made with organic ingredients

At least 70% must be from organic ingredients.

"Made with organic" must appear on the products and list up to three ingredients. The percentage of ingredients must also be listed.

Use of the "Organic" seal is prohibited.

Other Labeling Provisions

Products with less than 70% organic ingredients should not be listed as organic.

USDA Organic Seal

A seal has been developed by the USDA making it a federal requirement.

100% Organic

On October 21, 2002, the 100% organic seal became available. For a period of time you may see old labels, since producers are allowed to use the old seals until the supplies are all used up. It is up to retailers of organic stores to protect their integrity.

What the Labels Mean for Meat

Natural: With natural meat. It is processed with a minimum of synthetic chemicals. It is important to buy from a reliable organic store.

Free-farmed: This indicates that the animal was humanely raised, meaning the animals were allowed access to outdoor pasture, fresh air, and have not received hormones or antibiotics.

Nitrate-free: When it is stated on the label, nitrate-free means that no chemicals are used to speed up the growth and preserve the color of meat.

Chapter 3: Nutrition and Health

Nutrition: Is the way our body utilizes food.

Food: Is the product where we get our nutrients.

Nutrients: Are chemical substances in food that nourish the body.

TRANSITION INTO ORGANIC FOODS

The nutrients are:	Sources
Carbohydrates	bread, pasta
Fats	butter, avocado
Protein	chicken, tofu
Vitamins	whole-grain cereal, nuts
Minerals	spring water, rainwater

All essential nutrients needed by the body are available through food. The way food is handled determines the amount of nutrients it contains. It also determines its safety, quality, appearance, taste, acceptability, and cost.

Organic Foods and Ingredients

Here are just a few examples of organic foods you can find that cross into different cultures.

American foods:

    Hot dogs

    Rolls

    Salmon

    Asparagus

    Broccoli

    Potato chips

    Popcorn

    Tuna

    Orange juice

Latino foods:

    Tortillas

    Chili peppers

    Corn

    Chickpeas

    Figs

    Coffee

    Beans

    Seasonings

    Coconuts

    Mangoes

TRANSITION INTO ORGANIC FOODS

African-American foods:
- Pork
- Fish
- Chicken
- Potatoes
- Collard greens
- Rolls
- Beans
- Corn bread
- Watermelon
- Milk

Indian-American foods:
- Lentils
- Split peas
- Bread
- Curry
- Flour
- Potatoes

    Saffron

    Baking powder

    Thyme

    Hot sauce

Chinese-American foods:

    Rice

    Noodles

    Soy sauce

    Shrimp

    Corn oil

    Beef

    Soups

    Tofu

Japanese-American foods:

    Lobster

    Shrimp

    Watercress

TRANSITION INTO ORGANIC FOODS

    Tea

    Seaweed

    Soybeans

    Wasabi

    Sushi

    And so many more.

Below is a list of additional products you can purchase in your health food store. Please note there are a lot more products available than you see here. This is just to show that you can find these items in their organic form.

Fresh Produce

    Organic peppers

    Organic cabbage

    Organic carrots

    Organic onions

    Organic lettuce

    Organic potatoes

Organic tomatoes

Organic broccoli

Organic bananas

Organic grapefruit

Organic oranges

Organic apples

Organic peaches

Organic black plums

Baking Needs:

Organic wheat flour

Organic all-purpose flour – unbleached all purpose flour (no chemicals added)

Pasta and Rice:

Organic pastas

Organic macaroni and cheese

Organic arborio rice

Organic jasmine rice

TRANSITION INTO ORGANIC FOODS

    Organic sushi rice
    Organic brown rice
    Organic long-grain rice
    Organic pasta sauce

Dairy:
    Organic butter
    Organic cheese
    Organic tofu
    Organic rice milk
    Organic chocolate milk

Canned Foods:
    Organic baked beans
    Organic black beans
    Organic chili beans
    Organic garbanzo beans
    Organic pinto beans
    Organic red beans

Frozen Foods:
- Organic frozen vegetables
- Organic vegetable lasagna
- Organic meat-free burgers

Sauces:
- Organic Worcestershire
- Organic teriyaki
- Organic ginger
- Organic hot pepper
- Organic barbecue

Beverages
- Spring water
- Organic apple juice
- Organic soda

Dressings:
- Organic olive oil
- Organic canola oil

Organic mayonnaise

Organic vinegar

Organic Pleasures:

Organic ice cream

Organic cake

Organic pizza

Organic chips

Organic cheesecake

Organic chocolate

Washing Our Hands

An act that is so simple and yet so often forgotten is washing our hands. We wash our hands to prevent the spread of harmful bacteria. When washing your hands, use this procedure: First, wet your hands, then apply the soap. Lather well by rubbing hands together with fingers interlocking for ten to fifteen seconds, then rinse. Remember to use very warm water when washing and rinsing, dry hands with paper towel (as damp cloth towels can harbor germs). If you are out using a public facility, use a dry paper towel to turn off the running tap and to open the door to exit. This is a good way to prevent the spread of germs and to contribute to a cleaner environment.

How The Change In Health Care Will Force Us To Do What Is Right

The cost of health care has been going up every year for the last few years, and according to studies it will continue to increase. Some companies are raising premiums and some are asking us to switch to our spouse's health care plan. They are also giving incentives for those of us who do switch. For example, companies will offer an increase in pay and others will offer a bigger salary when you accept a position but opt out of their insurance coverage. This may work if you have a spouse who has a plan you can join, but it is very costly for single individuals who need health insurance coverage.

The concern is that we are either going to be dropped from insurance plans obtained through our employers, or our premiums will keep going up. If our health diminishes while insurance and health care costs go up, we are going to be faced with a serious health burden. Think about this for a minute. If we continue to eat conventional foods that we know are filled with harmful chemicals and pesticides, and don't get regular checkups, and we find our selves paying more for health care, wouldn't it be nice to avoid the unhealthy, costly vicious cycle and be healthy?

One way we can protect ourselves is to take care of our bodies right now. Eat well-balanced, organic meals free from manmade chemicals, get regular checkups, drink lots of water, and stay active.

How Can I Reach An Organic Certifying Agency That Serves My Area?

Depending on the area you live in, or the area you're interested in doing organic farming in, you can get information by contacting the National Organic Certifying Certifiers Directory [610-756-4026] or USDA National Organic Program [406-444-4687]. If you are in the Northeast area, contact Northeast

Organic Farming [518-734-5495] of New York or NOFA-NY.

Chapter 4: Basics

Conventional fruits and vegetables facts. I have listed some fruits and vegetables that are high and low in chemicals and pesticides.

Foods High in Pesticides

- Apples
- Apricots
- Bell peppers
- Celery
- Cherries
- Chili peppers
- Green beans
- Nectarines
- Pears
- Strawberries
- Spinach
- Tomatoes

Foods Low in Pesticides

- Avocado
- Bananas
- Blueberries
- Broccoli

TRANSITION INTO ORGANIC FOODS

Brussels sprouts

Cabbage

Cauliflower

Eggplant

Grapefruit

Kiwi

Mangoes

Okra

Asparagus

Onions

Papaya

Pineapples

Plums

Radishes

Watermelons

I have done two samples of grocery list one from conventional foods to mostly organic foods, showing you how you can transition. You will notice where one products can be substituted for another.

For example using Organic sesame sticks if you prefer instead of conventional potato chips.

Current Grocery List – (conventional foods)

Flounder per lb.	$8.99
Chicken(w/ Growth Hormone) per lb.	$5.29
5 cans of tuna ($.99 per can)	$4.95
Tofu	$1.50
Lettuce	$1.99
Tomatoes	$1.49
Broccoli ($.79 per lb.)	$1.58
Carrots ($.79 per lb.)	$2.13
2 cans of beans ($.79 per lb.)	$1.58
Potato chips	$1.09
2 loaves bread ($1.29 per bag)	$2.58
Pizza	$3.99
Bananas ($.69 per lb)	$2.42
Cereal	$3.49
3 containers yogurt ($.80 each)	$2.40

TRANSITION INTO ORGANIC FOODS

Mayonnaise	$1.99
1 pound butter	$2.50
1 gallon milk	<u>$3.09</u>
	$53.05

New Grocery List – (organic foods)

Grey sole (natural)	$4.47
Organic chicken tenderloin	$4.31
5 cans of tuna ($.99 each)	$4.95
Tofu	$1.29
Organic lettuce	$1.79
Organic tomatoes	$1.73
Organic broccoli ($1.98 per lb.)	$3.41
Organic carrots ($.86 per lb.)	$2.23
2 cans of organic beans ($1.09 each)	$2.18
Sesame sticks ($.98 per lb.)	$0.90
2 Organic bread ($2.29 each)	$3.58
Pizza made with organic ingredients	$3.69
Organic bananas ($.98 per lb.)	$3.42

Granola hemp ($.98 per lb.)	$2.94
3 containers organic yogurt ($.79 ea.)	$2.37
Mayonnaise w/organic ingredients	$1.99
1 pound butter	$2.19
1 gallon organic milk	<u>$4.89</u>
	$52.33

*Grey sole was on sale

*Coupon for organic bread $1.00

*Coupon for tofu $.40

*You can choose loose cereal (Granola Hemp) to bag and take home. It is less expensive, and tastes better, too.

Be Informed

Prices change constantly. Also, new items become available at lower prices. Coupons and offers can help. Since companies want customers to get familiar with their products, they often hold contests like cooking, offer lifestyle makeovers, and give free products away. There are coupons for items like bread, pasta sauce, tofu, and yogurt, just to list a few.

TRANSITION INTO ORGANIC FOODS

A great place to get coupons for organic foods is www.mambosprouts.com. Call 1-888-965-6262.

A Good Alternative

For many people with allergies, organic foods can be a great alternative. For example, the company Pacific Bakery makes yeast-free breads, wheat alternatives, goods baked with no sugar or honey, no eggs or dairy, no baking powder/soda, and they are 100% non-GMO (non-genetically modified organisms). There is a large selection of foods for your dietary needs. You can find dairy-free, gluten-free, low-fat, low-sodium, low-sugar or sugar-free, and soy (for those with milk allergies). Please consult with your physician.

Resources

These are some magazines and web sites where you can get more information on organics.

www.utne.com

www.naturalhealth.com

www.organicstyle.com

www.organicgardening.com

www.herbquarterly.com

www.motherearthnews.com

www.consciouschoice.com

Looking Beyond Organic Foods

Chemicals and pesticides are everywhere, in everything we eat and drink that is not organic. Start looking into taking care of other areas of your life. For example, there is a whole realm of skin care and household products available that can help you continue to eliminate the chemicals from your life, not only the ones you ingest, but also chemicals that you breathe and touch.

Chapter 5: Exercises for Your

Please do these exercises. They will help you with getting into organic foods.

On the following page there is a blank grocery list so that you can list the items you need, the date you are going to be picking up your new items, the most important items you will be starting with, and the prices. This will give you an idea of how much it will all cost.

Do whichever exercise you prefer to do first; you do not have to do them in the order presented here.

MY TRANSITION CALENDAR / MY NEW GROCERY LIST

GROCERY LIST	ACTION DATE	ITEMS TO START WITH	HOW MUCH WOULD IT COST

TRANSITION INTO ORGANIC FOODS

Another exercise for you

After purchasing organic foods and ingredients, eat the following breakfast, lunch, snack, and dinner for seven consecutive days. Record the results on the last day on the following page.

1. When did you first feel hungry after eating your meals?

2. How much food satisfied you and was it your normal portion size, or were you satisfied before you had completed the meal?

3. How did it taste?

4. Did you get a bloated feeling after eating?

5. How did you feel overall after eating organic foods?

6. What do you account for the differences in organic foods from conventional foods?

When You Do Your Shopping What is Most Important to You?

When purchasing foods, we should choose foods that will contribute to or promote good health. Below are some words for you to take a look at and see what is most important to you. Choose one:

o If it's organic   o Ounces

o Fat content   o Sodium

o Calories   o Potassium

TRANSITION INTO ORGANIC FOODS

- o If it is heavily processed (e.g., white flour vs. whole-grain flour)

- o Protein content

The answer should be all of the above but you might want to start with organic foods first, because you are now aware that organic foods do not contain harmful chemicals.

We need to do what is right for us first. Get rid of the harmful chemicals we ingest. By choosing organic, we are doing that, and then we can move on to the nutritional labels. For example, the protein content and fat content. What you choose to focus on after going organic depends on your needs. If you are on a regular diet, or if you have restrictions because of health issues, then you need to work with your doctor who, in turn, would recommend you to a nutritionist or someone qualified to help you choose the right/healthy meals for you to eat. Please consult with your physician.

Taste Test Organic Fruit Products

Scale:

    5 – Excellent; outstanding

    4 – Above satisfactory; prepared above standard expectation

    3 – Satisfactory; meets standards for taste

    2 – Acceptable; is edible but could taste better

    1 – Unacceptable; cannot be eaten

In this exercise, taste these different fruits and record the results in the appropriate column, using the rating scale above. I have included additional space so you may try fruits of your choice.

TRANSITION INTO ORGANIC FOODS

ITEMS	OVERALL APPEAR-ANCE	FLAVOR	TASTE	COLOR
APPLES				
GRAPES				
ORANGES				

Do a Three-day Taste Test

	SATURDAY	SUNDAY	MONDAY
BREAKFAST			
LUNCH			
SNACK			
DINNER			

TRANSITION INTO ORGANIC FOODS

Please use this grocery list column below to write out the grocery items you purchase so you can see the choices you have made. This will help you to move toward making your new grocery list.

My Actual Grocery List

ITEMS	PRICE

ITEMS	PRICE

Resources:

    WHOLE FOODS-SUPERMARKET

    WILD OATS-SUPERMARKET

    TRADER JOE'S - SUPERMARKET

    UTNE-MAGAZINE

    ORGANIC STYLE-MAGAZINE

TRANSITION INTO ORGANIC FOODS

This has been a life-changing experience for me within the transitions of my life and especially in the past few years. Changing my thinking toward eating organic foods has helped me learn how food is processed and how the conventional food industry operates. I feel I am a better person because of my learning experiences.

I am sharing some of the books that have helped me in becoming the person I am now.

ORGANIC GARDENING
By Maria Rodale

THE POWER OF NOW
By Eckhart Tolle

DISCOVER THE POWER WITH IN YOU
By Eric Butterworth

TRANSITION INTO ORGANIC FOODS
ORDER FORM
ISBN#: 0-9753061-0-3

Name: _____

Address: _____

City: _____

State: _____ Zip: _____

Quantity of books _____ @ $14.95 each $ _____

Shipping _____   @ $4.00 per book $ _____

Additional shipping   @ $1.00 per book $ _____

New Jersey residents, please add $.90 sales tax $ _____

Please make your check or money order payable to:

Lehcar Publishing

P.O. Box 408

Montclair, New Jersey 07042

Visit www.RachelValentin.com for secure online ordering